Highway to Heaven

56 *Gospel Favorites
for Choir, Congregation,
or Ensemble*

Usable in Medleys or Individually

Compiled and arranged by TOM FETTKE

Lillenas PUBLISHING COMPANY

KANSAS CITY, MO 64141

Highway to Heaven

Traditional
Arranged by Tom Fettk

FOR ETERNITY

includes
My Savior First of All
Ten Thousand Years

Medley arranged by Tom Fettke

Presentation Suggestions:
MY SAVIOR FIRST OF ALL: Choir parts with repeat, medley ending
TEN THOUSAND YEARS: Verse 1, choir unison; Refrain, parts, repeat ending; Verse
2, parts; Refrain, parts, medley ending

My Savior First of All

FANNY J. CROSBY

JOHN R. SWENEY
Arranged by Tom Fettke

Ten Thousand Years

Words and Music by
ELMER COLE

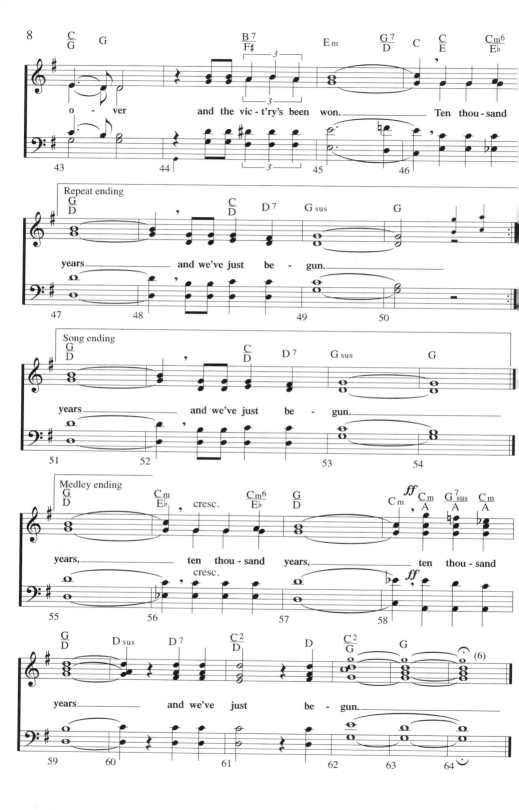

WALKING AND TALKING

includes

My Lord and I
I'm Gonna Keep Walking

Medley arranged by Tom Fettke

Presentation Suggestions:
MY LORD AND I: Choir parts, repeat as written, medley ending
I'M GONNA KEEP WALKING: Refrain, choir parts; Verse 1, solo, 1st ending;
Refrain, choir parts; Verse 2, solo, 2nd ending

My Lord and I

Traditional
Arranged by Tom Fettke

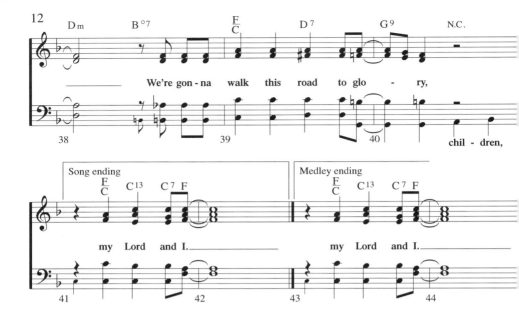

I'm Gonna Keep Walking

Words and Music by
JERRY THOMPSON
and NILES BOROP

Wherever You Are

Words and Music by
**JOYCE MARTIN MCCULLOUGH,
HARRIE MCCULLOUGH and JOEL LINDSEY**
Arranged by Tom Fettke

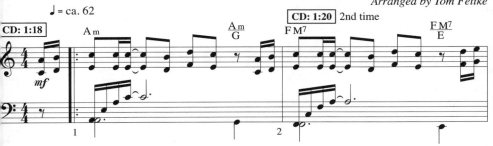

1st time: Choir unison
2nd time: Ladies unison

1. Are you stand-ing_____ at a cross-road_____ wond-'ring which road you should take? And you're
2. You are wait-ing_____ to hear thun-der_____ and see light-'ning in the sky._____ O but

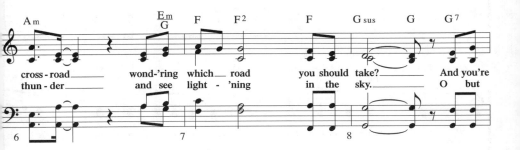

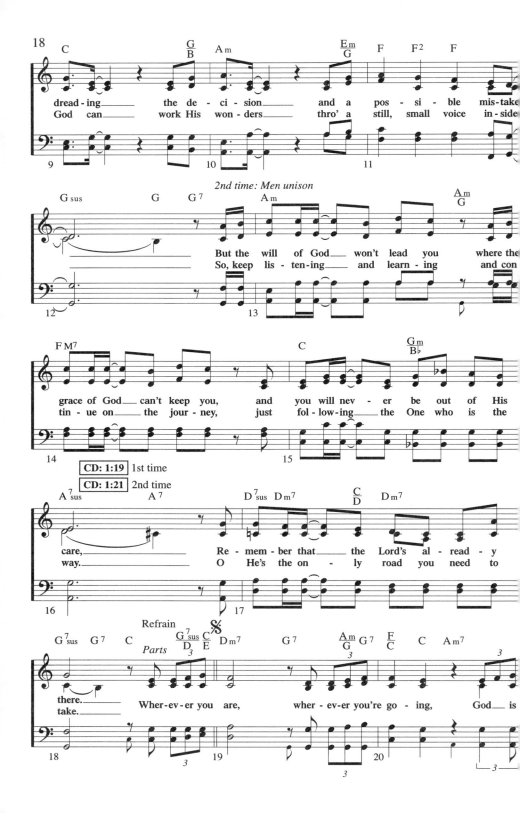

HIS GREAT LOVE

includes

Somebody Loves Me
Jesus Loves Me
Out of His Great Love

Medley arranged by Tom Fettke

Presentation Suggestions:
SOMEBODY LOVES ME: Verse 1, choir parts, verse repeat ending; Verse 2, choir
unison; Refrain, choir parts, refrain repeat ending; Refrain, unison, song ending
JESUS LOVES ME: 1st time, solo; 2nd time, solo with choir parts, medley ending
OUT OF HIS GREAT LOVE: Refrain, parts; Verse 1, ladies unison; Refrain, parts;
Verse 2, ladies unison, 2nd ending; Refrain, parts

Somebody Loves Me

Words and Music by
W. F. and MARJORIE CRUMLEY
Arranged by Tom Fettke

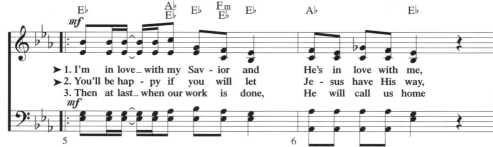

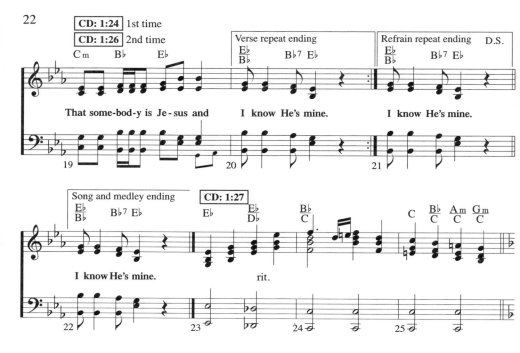

Jesus Loves Me

Words and Music by
V. B. (VEP) ELLIS
Arranged by Tom Fettke

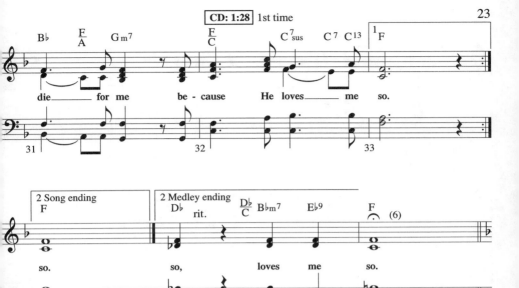

die____ for me be - cause He loves____ me so.

so. so, loves me so.

Out of His Great Love

Words and Music by
TERRY and BARBI FRANKLIN

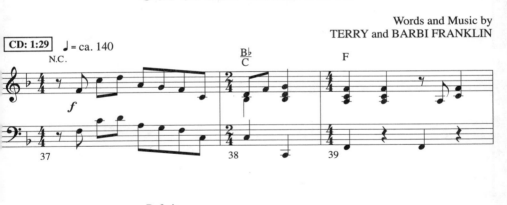

Out of His great love He picked me__ up,

GREAT AND WONDERFUL GOD

includes

O Lord, How Wonderful

Bigger than Any Mountain

Medley arranged by Tom Fettke

Presentation Suggestions:

O LORD, HOW WONDERFUL: Choir parts; Measure 14 beat 3, ladies unison; D.S., choir parts, coda-medley ending

BIGGER THAN ANY MOUNTAIN: Choir parts, medley ending

O Lord, How Wonderful

MOSIE LISTER
and KEN BIBLE

MOSIE LISTER
Arranged by Tom Fettke

Bigger than Any Mountain

Words and Music
GORDON JENSE

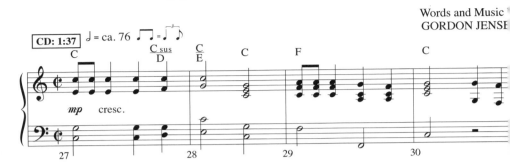

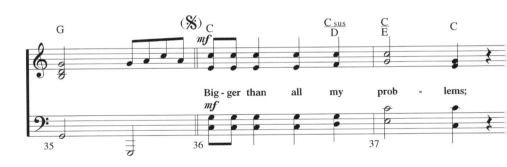

Big - ger than all my prob - lems;

Big - ger than all my fears; God is big - ger than an - y mo

30

JESUS IS HERE

includes
He's as Close as the Mention of His Name
He Is Here

Medley arranged by Tom Fettk

Presentation Suggestions:
HE'S AS CLOSE AS THE MENTION OF HIS NAME: Verse 1, choir unison; Refrain, parts, repeat ending; Verse 2, men unison; Measure 6, beat 4, ladies unison; Measure 8, beat 4, men unison; Measure 10, beat 4, ladies unison; Refrain, choir parts, medley ending
HE IS HERE: Choir unison, medley ending; Measure 46, parts, medley ending

He's as Close as the Mention of His Name

Words and Music b
GORDON JENSE

34

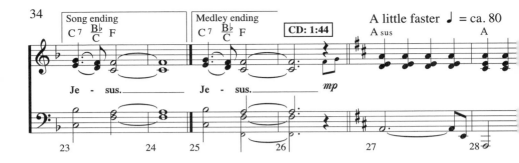

He Is Here

Words and Music by
KIRK TALLEY

here;   lis - ten   close - ly,   Hear   Him

call - ing out____ your   name.   He   is   here;   you   can

CD: 1:45

Song ending

touch Him,   You   will   nev - er   be   the   same.

Medley ending

cresc.

same.   cresc.   He   is   here,   hal - le -

lu - jah!   He   is   here,   a - men!   He   is

36

WONDERFUL IS HE

includes
Wonderful (Yandell)
My Wonderful Lord
Wonderful (Lillenas)

Medley arranged by Tom Fettke

Presentation Suggestions:
WONDERFUL (Yandell): Verse 1, choir parts; Refrain, parts, repeat ending; Verse 2, parts; Refrain, parts, medley ending
MY WONDERFUL LORD: Solo
WONDERFUL (Lillenas): Choir unison, medley ending; Measure 57, choir parts

Wonderful

JAMES ROWE and
P. J. ZONDERVAN

M. L. YANDELL

1. Won-der-ful is Je - sus, our match-less King.   Won-der-ful the praise which to
2. Won-der-ful is Je - sus, our com-ing King,   Hum-bly, at His feet,   we our

Him   we   sing;   Won-der-ful the friend   un-to   whom   we   cling,
trib - ute   bring;   "Wor-thy   is the Lamb"   we will   ev - er   sing!

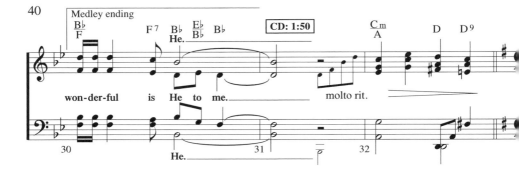

My Wonderful Lord

Words and Music by
HALDOR LILLENAS
Arranged by Tom Fettke

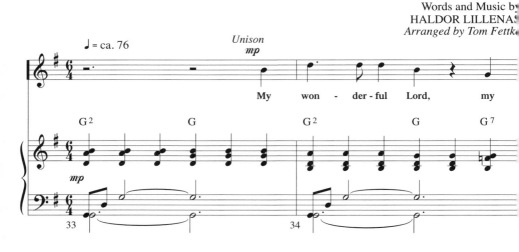

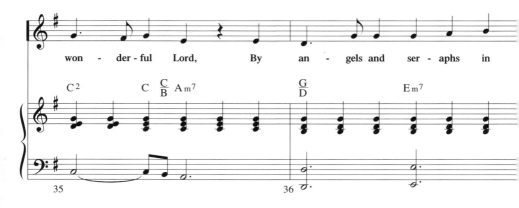

Wonderful

Words and Music by
HALDOR LILLENAS
Arranged by Tom Fettk

COME WITH YOUR BURDENS

includes

Leave It There

And He's Ever Interceding

Medley arranged by Tom Fettk

Presentation Suggestions:
LEAVE IT THERE: Parts, repeat as written
AND HE'S EVER INTERCEDING: Verse 1, ladies unison; Measure 35, choir unison;
Refrain, parts, repeat ending; Verse 2, solo; Refrain, choir parts, medley ending

Leave It There

Words and Music b
CHARLES ALBERT TINDLE
Arranged by Tom Fettk

And He's Ever Interceding

Words and Music b
CAROLYN GILLMA

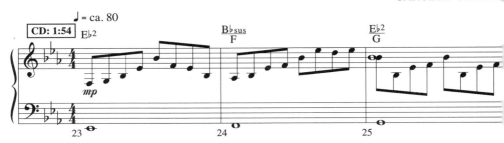

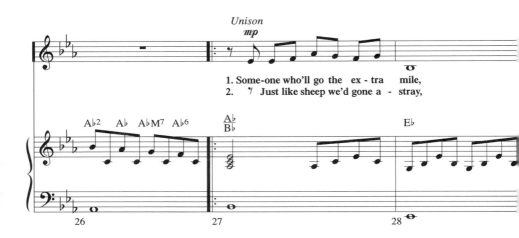

1. Some-one who'll go the ex - tra mile,
2. Just like sheep we'd gone a - stray,

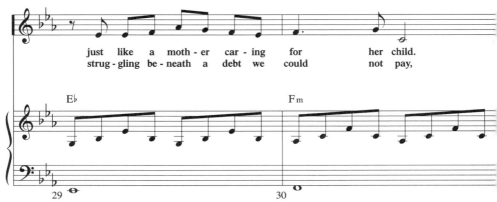

just like a moth - er car - ing for her child.
strug - gling be - neath a debt we could not pay,

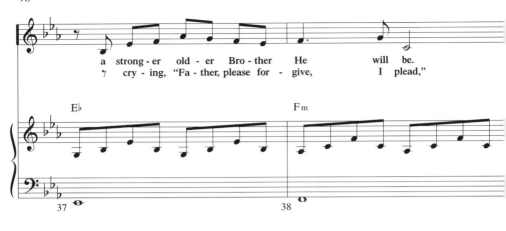

a strong - er old - er Bro - ther He will be.
cry - ing, "Fa - ther, please for - give, I plead,"

So quick and read - y to de - fend
And as the nails pierced in His hands

the young - er, weak - er, to the end.
God once a - gain reached out to man.

CD: 1:55 1st time
CD: 1:57 2nd time

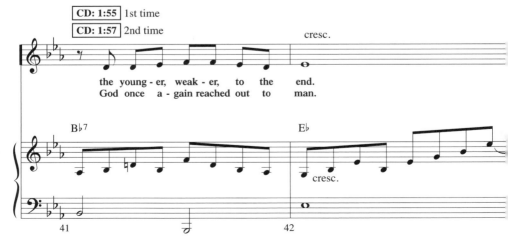

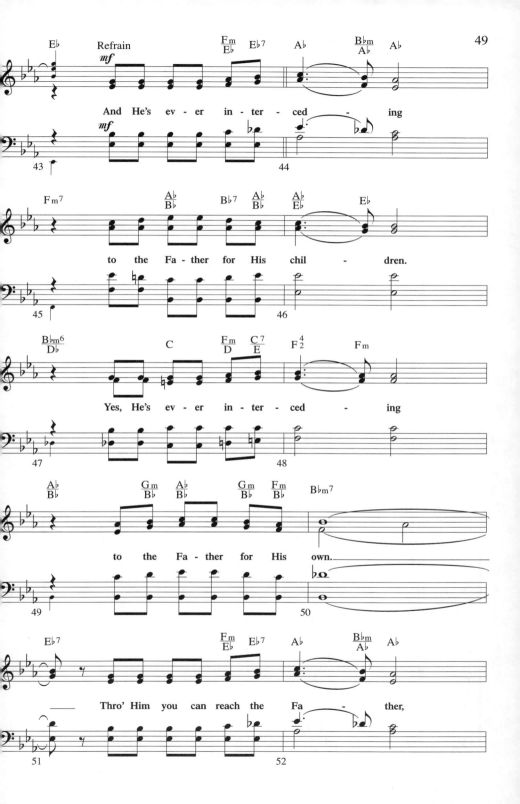

50

I Can See the Hand

Words and Music by
STEVEN CURTIS CHAPMAN
and JIM CHAPMAN III
Arranged by Tom Fettke

52

53

NAME ABOVE ALL NAMES

includes
Speak His Name
What a Lovely Name

Medley arranged by Tom Fettke

Presentation Suggestions:
SPEAK HIS NAME: Refrain, choir part; Verse 1, unison, D.S.; Refrain, parts, coda-
medley ending
WHAT A LOVELY NAME: Verse 1; choir parts; Refrain, parts, repeat ending; Verse 2,
ladies parts; Refrain, choir parts, medley ending, solo/parts as indicated

Speak His Name

Words and Music by
MOSIE LISTER
Arranged by Tom Fettke

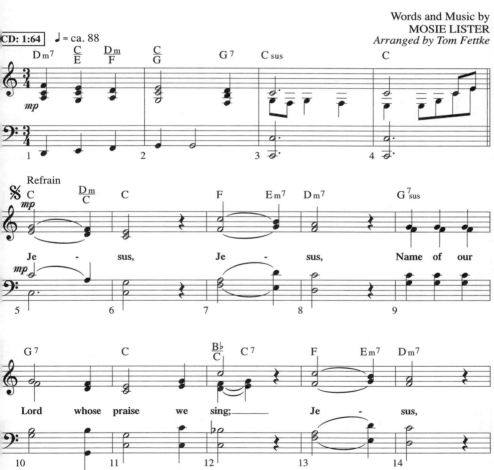

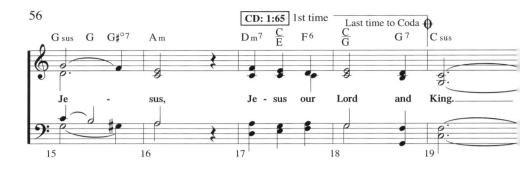

CD: 1:65 1st time

Last time to Coda

Je - sus, Je - sus our Lord and King.

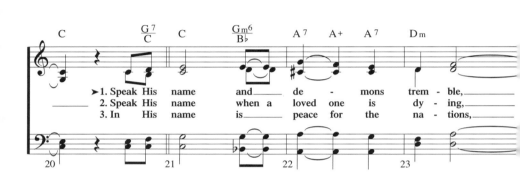

➤1. Speak His name and de - mons trem - ble,
2. Speak His name when a loved one is dy - ing,
3. In His name is peace for the na - tions,

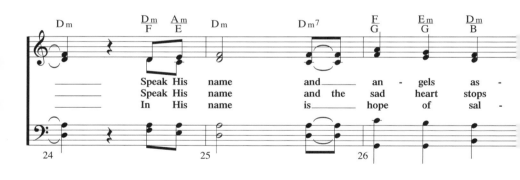

Speak His name and an - gels as -
Speak His name and the sad heart stops
In His name is hope of sal -

sem - ble. Speak His name and
cry - ing; Speak His name and
va - tion; In His name the

C C7 F6 F♯°7 B/F♯ F♯°7
mul - ti - tudes bow in awe And
glad hearts sing to - geth - er; A -
wan - der - er tossed and driv - en Finds
30 31 32
CD: 1:66
C/G G7 C D.S. al Coda
rev - 'rence be - fore His throne.
dor - ing be - fore His throne.
com - fort and peace un - known.
33 34 35 36
CODA Song ending
C sus rit. C
King.
CODA Medley ending
C sus rit. C
King.
A♭7 G♭/A♭ A♭
accel.
37 38 39 40 41

What a Lovely Name

Words and Music by
CHARLES B. WYCUFF

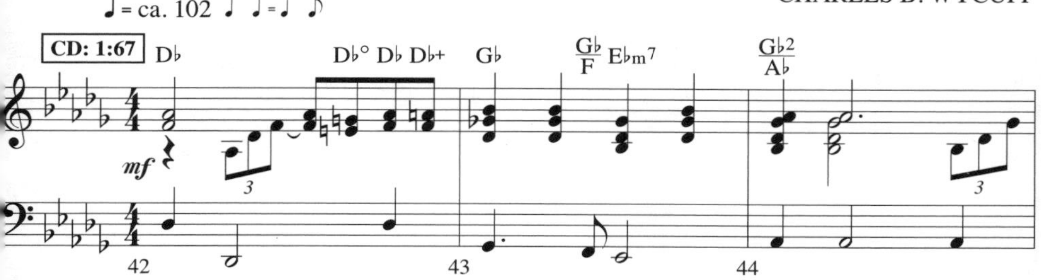
♩ = ca. 102
CD: 1:67
D♭ D♭° D♭ D♭+ G♭ G♭/F E♭m7 G♭2/A♭
mf
42 43 44

58

1. There's a name a-bove all oth-ers,
2. Through His name there's won-drous pow-er,
3. He'll re-turn in clouds of glo-ry,

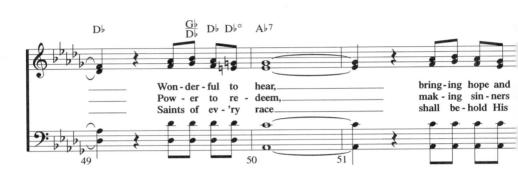

Won-der-ful to hear, bring-ing hope and
Pow-er to re-deem, mak-ing sin-ners
Saints of ev-'ry race shall be-hold His

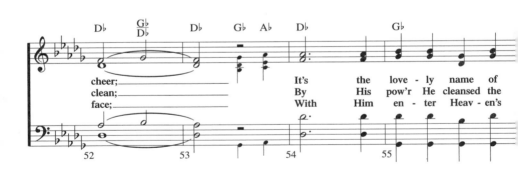

cheer; It's the love-ly name of
clean; By His pow'r He cleansed the
face; With Him en-ter Heav-en's

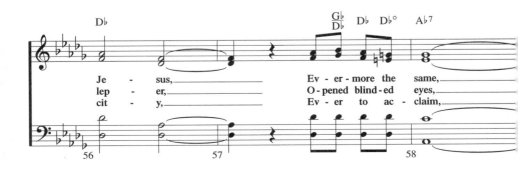

Je - sus, Ev-er-more the same,
lep - er, O-pened blind-ed eyes,
cit - y, Ev-er to ac-claim,

what a love-ly name!
caused the dead to rise.
"What a love-ly name!"

Refrain

What a love-ly name, this name of Je - sus,

Reach-ing high-er far than the bright-est

star; Sweet - er than the

songs they sing in Heav - en, Let the world pro-

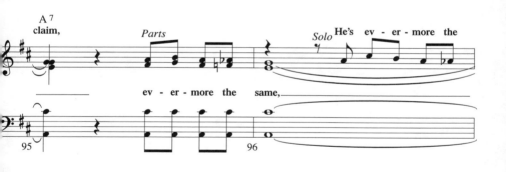

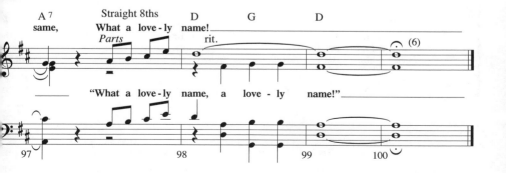

PRAISE THE NAME OF THE LORD

includes
Lift Him Up
Magnify Him

Medley arranged by Tom Fet

Presentation Suggestions:
LIFT HIM UP: Verse 1, choir unison, repeat ending; Verse 2, parts, medley ending
MAGNIFY HIM: Ladies unison; Measure 35 beat 3, men unison, medley ending;
Measure 44, choir parts

Lift Him Up

Words and Music
REBA RAM

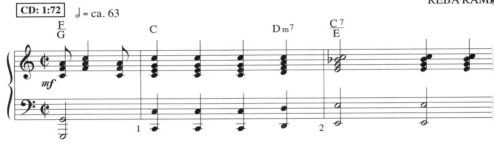

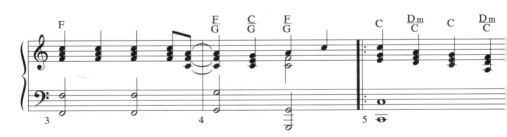

Magnify Him

RANDY VADER
and KIRK TALLEY

KIRK TALLEY

FAITHFUL AND TRUE

includes

He's All I Need

My Redeemer Is Faithful and True

Medley arranged by Tom Fettke

Presentation Suggestions:
   HE'S ALL I NEED: Verse 1, choir parts, repeat ending; Verse 2, choir unison, medley
   ending; Verse 3, choir parts
   MY REDEEMER IS FAITHFUL AND TRUE: Verse 1, ladies unison; Refrain, choir
   parts, 1st ending; Verse 2, solo; Refrain, choir parts, 2nd ending

He's All I Need

Traditional and
KEN BIBLE

Tradition
Arranged by Tom Fett

My Redeemer Is Faithful and True

Words and Music by
STEVEN CURTIS CHAPMAN
and JAMES ISAAC ELLIOTT

CROWN HIM SAVIOR AND KING

includes
I'm So Glad Jesus Lifted Me
Crown Him King

Medley arranged by Tom Fettke

Presentation Suggestions:
I'M SO GLAD JESUS LIFTED ME: Verse 1, choir unison, repeat ending; Verse 2,
choir parts, medley ending; Verse 3, parts
CROWN HIM KING: Verse 1, parts, repeat ending; Verse 2, parts, refrain repeat
ending; Refrain, song and medley ending

I'm So Glad Jesus Lifted Me

Traditional and
CAMP KIRKLAND

Traditional
Arranged by Tom Fettke

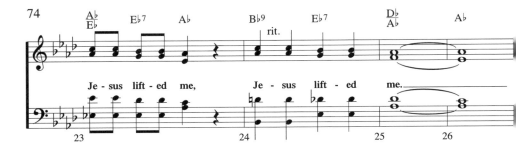

Crown Him King

LUTHER G. PRESLEY

WALLACE VARNER

76

HEAVEN'S CHILD

includes

I Belong to the King of the Ages
Child of the King
I've Been Adopted

Medley arranged by Tom Fettke

Presentation Suggestions:
I BELONG TO THE KING OF THE AGES: Verse 1, choir unison; Refrain, parts,
refrain repeat ending; Refrain, parts, medley ending
CHILD OF THE KING: Verse 1, choir parts; Refrain, parts, repeat ending; Verse 2,
ladies unison; Measure 61 beat 3, men unison; Refrain, choir parts, medley ending
I'VE BEEN ADOPTED: Choir parts, repeat ending, medley ending

I Belong to the King of the Ages

Words and Music by
STEPHEN R. ADAMS
Arranged by Tom Fettke

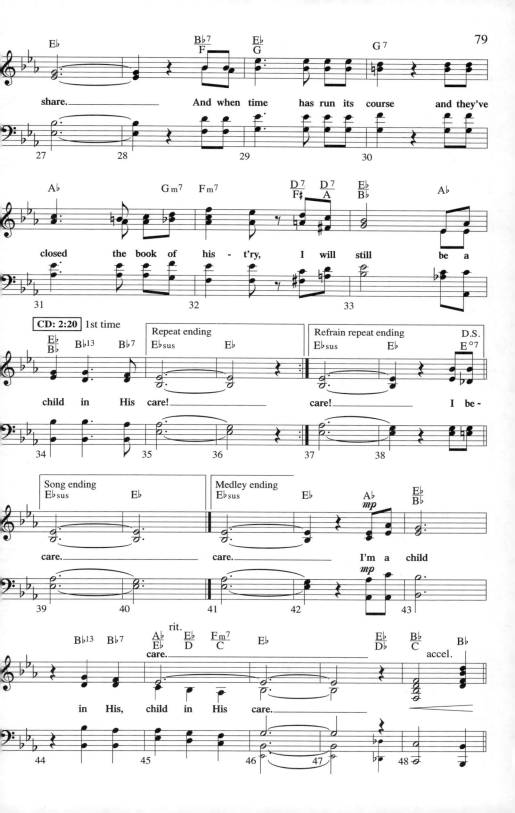

Child of the King

Words and Music b
CINDY WALKE

82

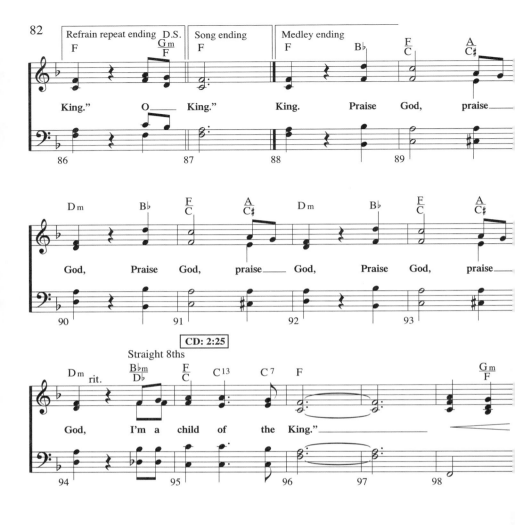

I've Been Adopted

Words and Music
STEPHEN R. ADAM
Arranged by Tom Fett

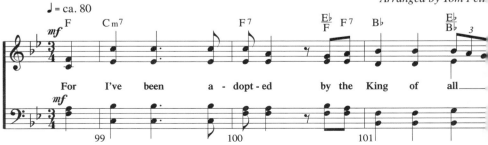

These Are They

WILLIAM J. and GLORIA GAITHER

WILLIAM J. GAITHER
Arranged by Tom Fettke

86

SAVED BY GRACE

includes

Sinner Saved by Grace
I Will Arise and Go to Jesus
Shoutin' Time

Medley arranged by Tom Fettke

Presentation Suggestions:
SINNER SAVED BY GRACE: Verse 1, choir parts; Refrain, parts, repeat ending; Verse
2, solo; Refrain, parts, medley ending
SHOUTIN' TIME/I WILL ARISE AND GO TO JESUS: Verse 1, ladies unison;
Refrain, choir parts, repeat ending; Verse 2, ladies unsion; Refrain, choir parts,
medley ending

Sinner Saved by Grace

GLORIA GAITHER

WILLIAM J. GAITHER
and MITCH HUMPHRIES

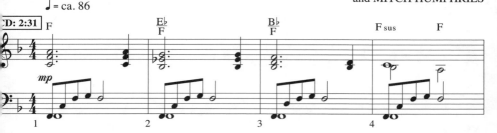

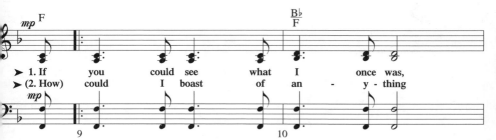

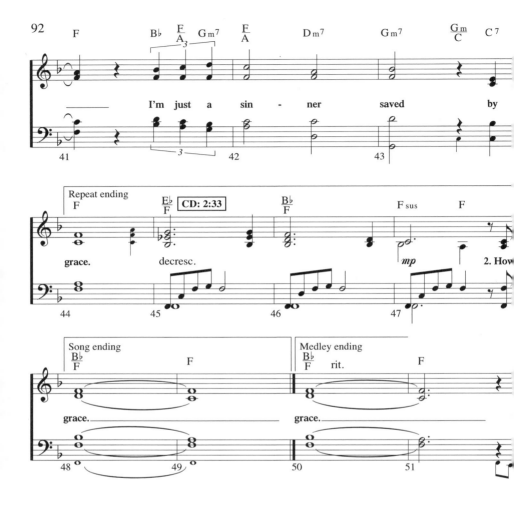

Shoutin' Time

with

I Will Arise and Go to Jesus

Traditio[n]

Arranged by Camp Kirkla[nd]
and Tom Fet[t]

*"I Will Arise and Go to Jesus"

94

CD: 2:36 1st time
CD: 2:38 2nd time

thou - sand charms.
love and pow'r.

It's shout - in' time in Heav - en, a sin - ner once lost is found, It's

shout - in' time in Heav - en, sal - va - tion has been bro't down. No

won - der the an - gels re - joice to know my sins have been cov - ered by the

crim - son flow and now I'm feel - in' fine, I'm

WE'LL RISE TO MEET HIM

includes
Coming Again
In the Twinkling of an Eye

Medley arranged by Tom Fett

Presentation Suggestions:
COMING AGAIN: Verse 1, choir unison, repeat ending; Verse 3, parts, medley ending
IN THE TWINKLING OF AN EYE: Verse 1, choir unison; Refrain, parts, repeat
ending; Verse 2, solo; Refrain, choir parts, medley ending

Coming Again

Words and Music
MOSIE LISTE
Arranged by Tom Fett

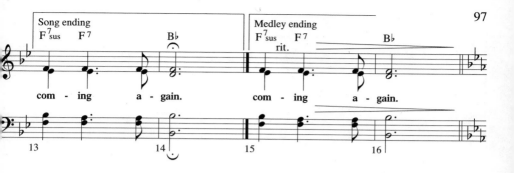

In the Twinkling of an Eye

Words and Music by
TIM GREENE

➤1. There's an awe - some feel - ing blow - ing, I can
➤2. Lit - tle chil - dren won't be cry - ing, Bro - ken

tell some - bod - y's com - ing; It's a
hearts won't be sigh - ing; God Him -

98

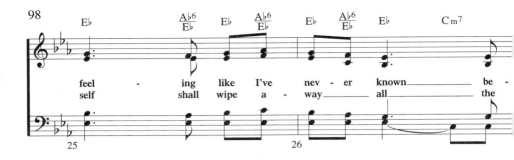

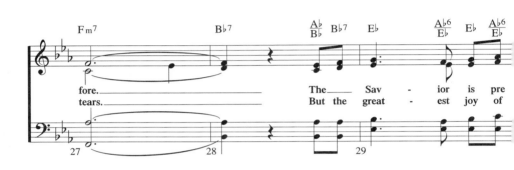

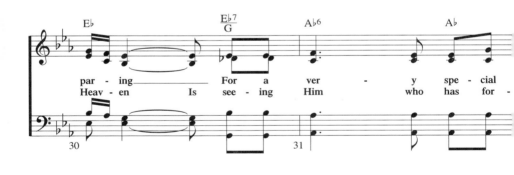

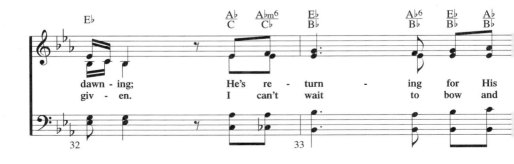

Jesus Saves

Words and Music by
ROGER and DEBBIE BENNETT
Arranged by Tom Fettke

102

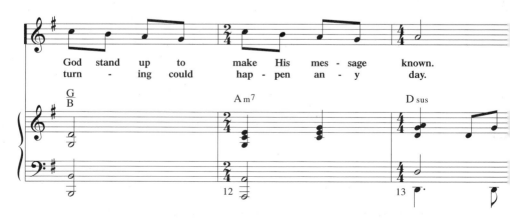

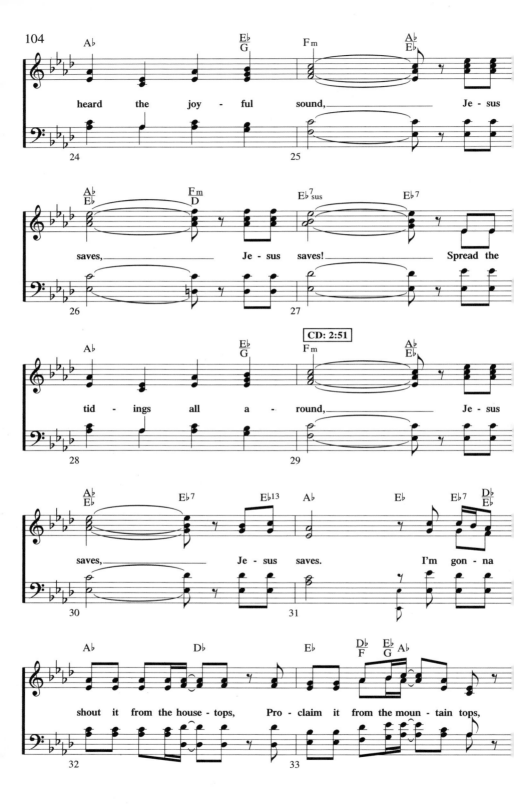

BY HIS STRIPES WE ARE HEALED

includes

He Has Surely Borne Our Sorrow

The Healer

Medley arranged by Tom Fett

Presentation Suggestions:
  HE HAS SURELY BORNE OUR SORROW: Verse 1, parts; Refrain, parts, repeat
  ending; Verse 3, choir unison, *mf*; Refrain, parts, medley ending
  THE HEALER: Verse 1, ladies unison; Measure 53, beat 3, men unison; Refrain, parts,
  repeat ending; Verse 2, choir unison; Refrain, parts, medley ending

He Has Surely Borne Our Sorrow

Words and Music
MOSIE LISTER
Arranged by Tom Fett

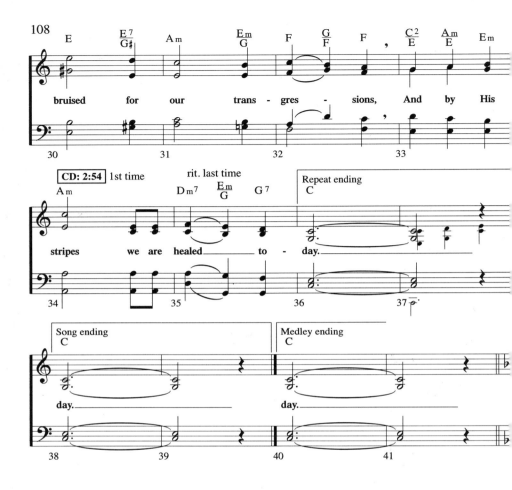

The Healer

Words and Music
LOIS IRW

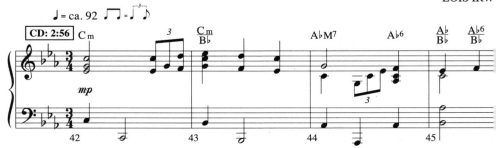

110

GLORIOUS PEACE

includes
Peace in the Midst of the Storm
Wonderful Peace
Peace like a River

Medley arranged by Tom Fettke

Presentation Suggestions:
PEACE IN THE MIDST OF THE STORM: Choir parts, 1st and 2nd endings
WONDERFUL PEACE: 1st time, solo, 1st ending; 2nd time, choir parts with solo, 2nd ending
PEACE LIKE A RIVER: Verse 1 and refrain, choir parts, repeat ending; Verse 2 and refrain, parts, medley ending

Peace in the Midst of the Storm

Words and Music by
STEPHEN R. ADAMS
Arranged by Tom Fettke

Wonderful Peace

Words and Music
HALDOR LILLEN
Arranged by Tom Fe

Db	D°7 G/D	D°7	Ab/Eb	Ab	Ab/Gb	F7	

Since my Re - deem - er has ran-somed my soul I have

28   29   30

CD: 2:62   1st time

Bbsus Bb   Eb7   1. Ab   Ab7   Db/Ab   Ab peace.   2. Ab   Ab7   Db/Ab   Ab peace.

peace,___ peace,   won - der - ful peace.   won - der - ful peace.

31   32 peace.___   33 peace.___

CD: 2:63

Ab   Bb/Ab   Gm7   Bb/C   C

accel.

34   35   36   37

Peace like a River

. B. WALBERT   JAMES D. WALBERT

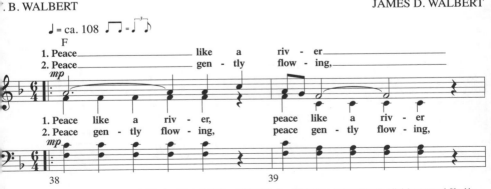

♩ = ca. 108

F

1. Peace___ like a riv - er___
2. Peace___ gen - tly flow - ing,___

mp

1. Peace like a riv - er, peace like a riv - er
2. Peace gen - tly flow - ing, peace gen - tly flow - ing,

mp

38   39

114

CD: 2:64 1st time
CD: 2:66 2nd time

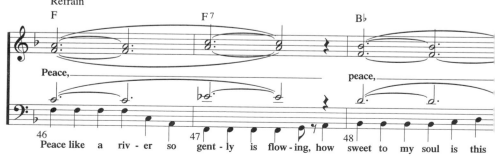

I'M GLAD I KNOW

includes

I'm Glad I Know Who Jesus Is
Yes, I Know!
O the Blood of Jesus

Medley arranged by Tom Fettke

Presentation Suggestions:
    I'M GLAD I KNOW WHO JESUS IS: Verse 1, choir unison; Refrain, parts, 1st
    ending; Verse 2, parts; Refrain, parts, 2nd ending, medley ending
    YES, I KNOW!: Verse 1, trio; Refrain, choir parts, repeat ending; Verse 3, trio; Refrain,
    choir parts, medley ending
    O THE BLOOD OF JESUS: Parts, medley ending

I'm Glad I Know Who Jesus Is

Words and Music by
GERON DAVIS

Yes, I Know!

Words and Music
ANNA W. WATERM
Arranged by Tom Fer

121

122

O the Blood of Jesus

Tradition.
Arranged by Tom Fett

RESTORE THE JOY

includes

Restore My Soul
There Is Joy in My Soul

Medley arranged by Tom Fettke

Presentation Suggestions:
RESTORE MY SOUL: Verse 1, choir unison; Refrain, parts, repeat ending; Verse 2,
ladies unison; Measure 14, beat 4, men unison; Refrain, choir parts, medley ending
THERE IS JOY IN MY SOUL: Verse 1, parts; Refrain, parts, repeat ending; Verse 3,
choir unison; Refrain, parts, medley ending

Restore My Soul

Words and Music by
MOSIE LISTER
Arranged by Tom Fettke

Medley Sequence copyright © 2000 by Pilot Point Music (ASCAP). All rights reserved.
Administered by The Copyright Company, 40 Music Square East, Nashville, TN 37203.

There Is Joy in My Soul

FANNY CROSBY

PAUL FERR
Arranged by Tom Fe

127

HEAVEN'S ENDLESS REFRAIN

Featuring the Refrains from the following Gospel Favorites:

Celebrate His Coming
We Shall See the King
Heaven's Jubilee
We Shall Rise
When the Saints Go Marching In
Everybody Will Be Happy Over There
When We All Get to Heaven
I'll Leave It All Behind
Goodby, World, Goodby

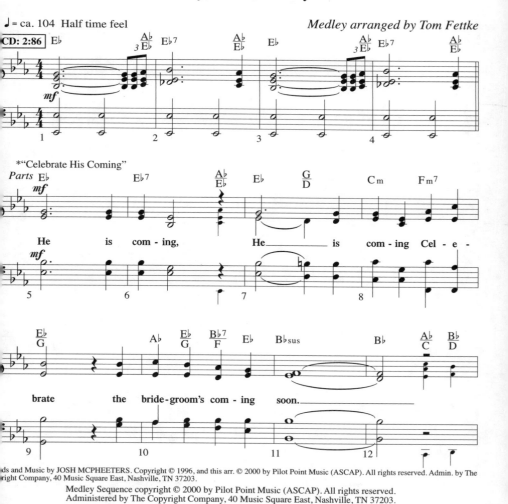

130

132

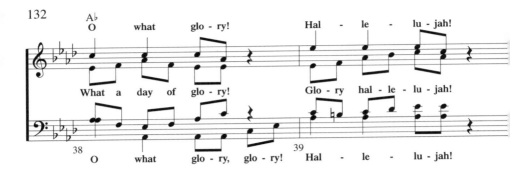

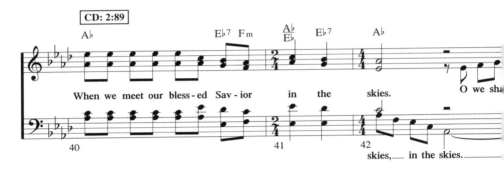

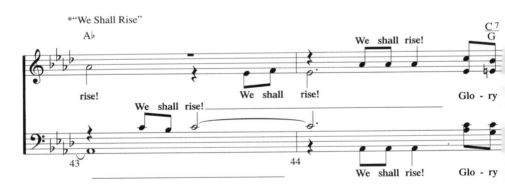

A little faster ♩ = ca. 126

Unison
f

O when the

D sus   D   G

accel.

55   56   57

*"When the Saints Go Marching In"

saints   go march-ing in,   O when the saints   go   march - ing

G

f

58   59   60

in!   O   I   want   to   be   in   that

D   G   G/F

61   62

ds and Music by E. M. BARTLETT. Arr. © 2000 by Pilot Point Music (ASCAP). All rights reserved. Admin. by The Copyright Company, 40
Square East, Nashville, TN 37203.

136

sing His praise; Ev - 'ry - bod - y will be hap - py o - ver

nev - er end - ing a - ges. Bod - y will be hap - py o - ver

*"When We All Get to Heaven"

there. When we all_____ get to

there.

heav - en, What a day of re - joic - ing that will be! When w

all see Je - sus, We'll sing and shout the vic - to

ry. decresc. Down here I

138

glo - ry _____ And my e - ter - nal home

*"Goodby, World, Goodby"

Now don't you weep for me when I'm

gone, 'Cause I won't have to leave here a

lone; And when I hear that last trum - pet

sound, My feet won't stay on the ground. _____ Gon - na

Medley Index

Topical Index

Alphabetical Index